Energy from Wind and Water

DONNA BAILEY

1991

STECK-VAUGHN
LIBRARY
A Division of Steck Vaughn Company
Austin, Texas

How to Use This Book

This book tells you many things about wind and water power. There is a Table of Contents on the next page. It shows you what each double page of the book is about. For example, pages 12 and 13 tell you about "Waterwheels."

On most of these pages you will find some words that are printed in **bold** type. The bold type shows you that these words are in the Glossary on pages 46 and 47. The Glossary explains the meaning of some words that may be new to you.

At the very end of the book there is an Index. The Index tells you where to find certain words in the book. For example, you can use it to look up words like hydroelectric power, reservoir, turbine, and many other words to do with wind and water power.

Library of Congress Cataloging-in-Publication Data

Bailey, Donna.
  Energy from wind and water / written by Donna Bailey.
    p. cm.—(Facts about)
  Includes index.
  Summary: Describes different methods of getting energy from wind or water, including windmills, waterwheels, dams, and the harnessing of river power.
  ISBN 0-8114-2519-3
  1. Wind power—Juvenile literature. 2. Water-power—Juvenile literature. [1. Wind power. 2. Water power.] I. Title.
II. Series: Facts about (Austin, Tex.)
TJ820.B35 1990   90-39388
621.2—dc20   CIP AC

Printed and bound in the United States of America
  2 3 4 5 6 7 8 9 0 LB 95 94 93 92

Contents

Introduction

You can see and feel **energy** as heat, light, and movement and it can change from one form of power to another. When wood burns, the energy stored in it changes into heat and light. People and animals get energy from food and turn it into movement. The picture shows how energy is used throughout the world.

coal

oil

natural gas

wood and plants

other sources of energy

Sun

water

water

Earth's heat

wind

Energy is stored in coal, food,
oceans and rivers, or in the Sun.

The windsurfer in the picture is
using a lot of energy. He has gained
this energy from the food he has
eaten. He is using the energy in his
body to balance on the board, and the
energy from the wind fills the sail.
He uses the energy from the top
of the waves to go faster through
the surf.

Where Energy Comes From

oil

natural gas

We get energy in many different ways.

We burn **fossil fuels** for energy.
We get oil and natural gas from wells
which we drill through the rocks.
We dig coal from underground mines.

Geothermal energy comes from the
hot rocks buried deep in the Earth.

We use these forms of energy for
heating and cooking and for factories,
machines, and **transportation.**

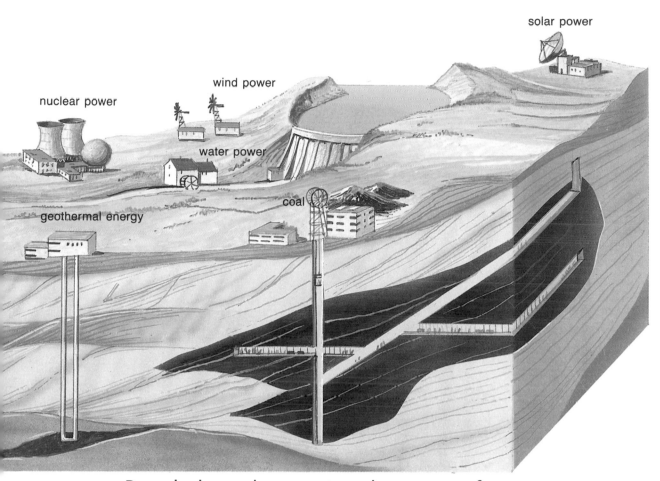

solar power

nuclear power

wind power

water power

geothermal energy

coal

People have been using the energy from wind and water for hundreds of years. We collect the Sun's energy in **solar power** stations, as well as getting energy from **nuclear power** stations. These are forms of **renewable** energy.

In about 60 years time, fossil fuels from under the ground will be used up. Scientists are trying to find new ways of using the power in wind and water.

Winds

Warm air is lighter than cool air.
At the **Equator** the weather is always
warm, but in the Arctic regions the
weather is always cold.

The diagram shows how the hot air at
the Equator rises into the **atmosphere.**
Cooler air from the North and South
Poles moves in to take its place.
As the warm air rises it gets cool,
so the air flows around and around.
The flow of air causes winds to blow.

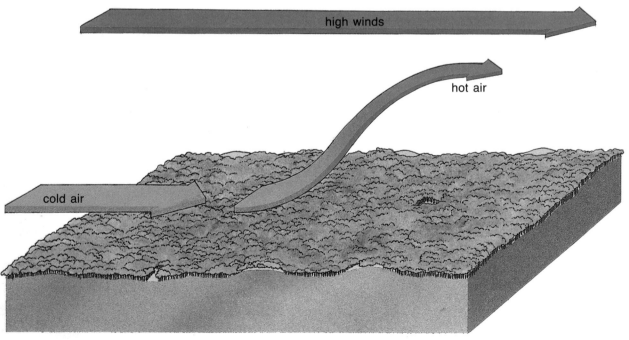

high winds

hot air

cold air

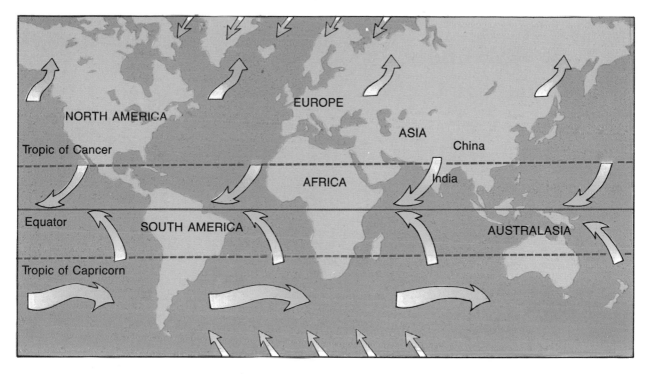

Winds blow in one direction for much of the year. You can see these wind patterns on the map.

The map shows **trade winds** from the northeast between the Tropic of Cancer and the Equator. Southeast trade winds blow between the Tropic of Capricorn and the Equator.

During a storm or **hurricane** the wind can do a lot of damage to houses.

hurricane damage along the coast

Windmills

Farmers built the first windmills in the Middle East about 1,300 years ago. They used windmills to lift river water onto the land.

Later they used **horizontal windmills** to grind corn. The wind blew into the mill through slits in the walls and turned the cloth sails of the windmills.

a windmill in Crete

The sails were fastened to a main **shaft** that went up through the ceiling and turned the heavy **millstone.**

a horizontal mill

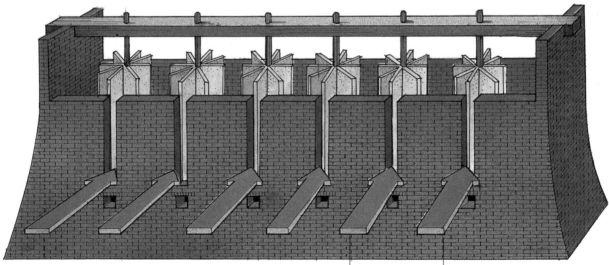

wind

About 800 years ago people in Europe
began to build **vertical mills.**

On the right side of the picture of a
wooden mill you can see the heavy stone
millstone used to grind corn into flour.
The sails of the windmill are on the
outside of the building. They are linked
to the millstone by the heavy main shaft
and the gear wheel.

The earliest vertical mill was built on
a thick post so the miller could turn
the whole mill around to face the wind.

11

Waterwheels

The picture shows huge waterwheels which are turned by water from
the Asi River in Syria.

The waterwheels use the power of
water to make electricity. The electricity
is used to power pumps that supply
water to nearby houses.

There are three kinds of waterwheels.

An undershot wheel is when the water in a river pushes the blades from below. It is used in slow-moving rivers.

An overshot wheel is when the water shoots over the top of the wheel from above, turning the blades as it falls. It works best in fast-flowing rivers.

A breastshot wheel is when the water hits and turns the blades in the middle of the wheel.

Waterwheels were used to grind corn and to make machines move in factories.

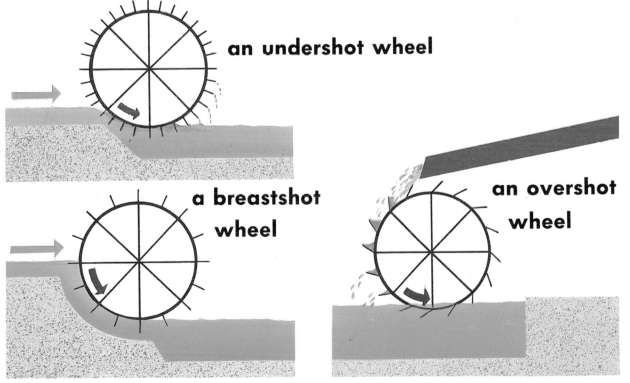

an undershot wheel

a breastshot wheel

an overshot wheel

Using Waterwheels

The picture shows farmers bringing
sacks of grain to the water mill.
The huge wheels under the mill turn the
millstones to grind the corn into flour.

   People also used waterwheels to
crush chalk and rocks to make roads.
Blacksmiths used waterwheels to lift
their heavy hammers.

Ioan. Stradanus invent.   Phls Galle excud.

a sawmill in Canada

Waterwheels go on working as long as there is enough water to turn the wheel.

A **weir** built across a river holds the water back and makes a mill pond. In dry weather when the level of the water in the stream drops the miller uses water in the pond to make the water flow faster.

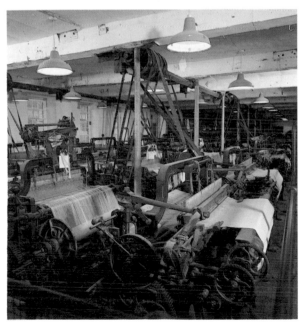

these weaving machines use power from waterwheels

The Water Cycle

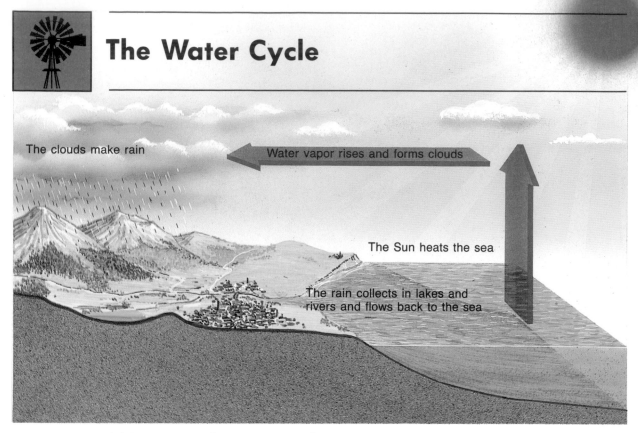

The clouds make rain

Water vapor rises and forms clouds

The Sun heats the sea

The rain collects in lakes and rivers and flows back to the sea

Water is always on the move.
The Sun heats the lakes and seas.
The water **evaporates** and rises up into
the atmosphere as water **vapor.**
The water vapor cools and forms clouds.
When the clouds go over the land the
vapor forms into drops that fall as
rain or snow. The rain runs into pools
and streams that flow downhill and
make rivers. The rivers flow into the
sea and the cycle begins all
over again.

Falling water is very powerful.
The power in this waterfall has cut a
deep valley in the rocks.

We use the power and energy in
moving water to produce electricity.

Building Dams

building the Itaipu Dam on the Paraná River

A dam in a river holds back the water to stop it from flowing. The water behind the dam makes a **reservoir.** The weight of all this water presses against the dam wall. The dam wall must be strong enough to stand up against this huge pressure.

the Itaipu dam is now nearly finished and so the reservoir has filled up

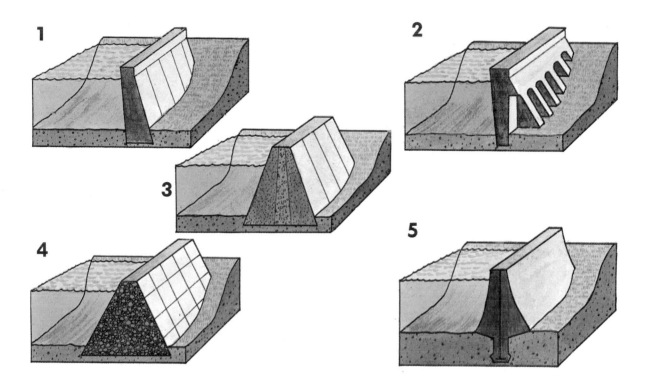

1. This dam has a solid concrete wall.

2. This buttress dam needs less concrete than a solid dam. The buttresses slope backward to strengthen the dam wall.

3. This dam wall is filled with clay and other waterproof material which stop the water from seeping through.

4. This dam wall is filled with rocks. The sides are lined with concrete or steel plates.

5. This dam wall has steel **foundations** which are sunk deep into the riverbed.

Electricity from Wind and Water

A **turbine** is a kind of wheel with many curved blades. Water flowing through a turbine pushes the blades around, making a **generator** turn to produce electricity.

reservoir

dam

sluice gates

water

generator

shaft

turbine

blades

a water turbine

Electricity that is produced by the turning of water turbines is called **hydroelectric power.** The water flows along a shaft into the turbine from **sluice gates** in the dam.

a wind generator

Windmills are a simple kind of wind turbine. They work like a turbine, but much more slowly.

Modern wind generators have special blades like propellers which spin very fast in the wind to generate electricity.

generators inside the power house beneath the Itaipu Dam

Water Power

Hydroelectric power stations are
built in the mountains where
there are waterfalls and fast-flowing
rivers.

The picture shows how we can control
the speed of water flowing in a river
by using a **spillway.**

In Canada there is a huge hydroelectric
system called the Kitimat Project.
The water behind the Kenney Dam falls
through a tunnel in Mount DuBose.
Engineers built the Kenamo Power
Station inside the mountain.
Pylons carry cables that take power
from the power station to Kitimat.

Hydroelectric Power

The yellow parts of the map show which countries produce the most hydroelectric power. These countries have high mountains and long rivers. The bar graph shows that the United States uses more hydroelectricity than any other country in the world.

The chart below shows which are the highest, the biggest, and the longest dams in the world, and what they are made of.

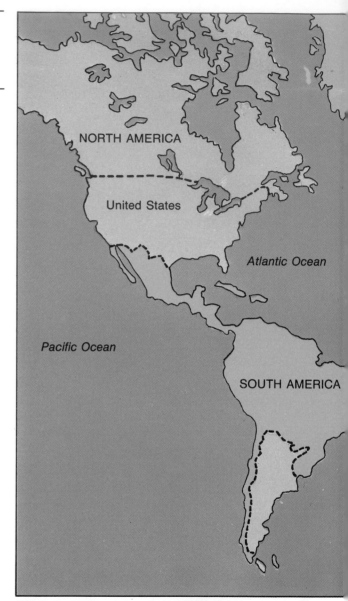

The Highest, Biggest, Longest Dams in the World				
	Name of dam	*Country*	*Measurements*	*Type*
Tallest dams	Rogun	Soviet Union	1,100 ft. high	rock
	Nurek	Soviet Union	1,040 ft. high	rock
	Grande Dixence	Switzerland	935 ft. high	concrete
Largest dams	Tarbela	Pakistan	5 billion cubic ft.	earth
	Fort Peck	U.S.A.	3.3 billion cubic ft.	earth

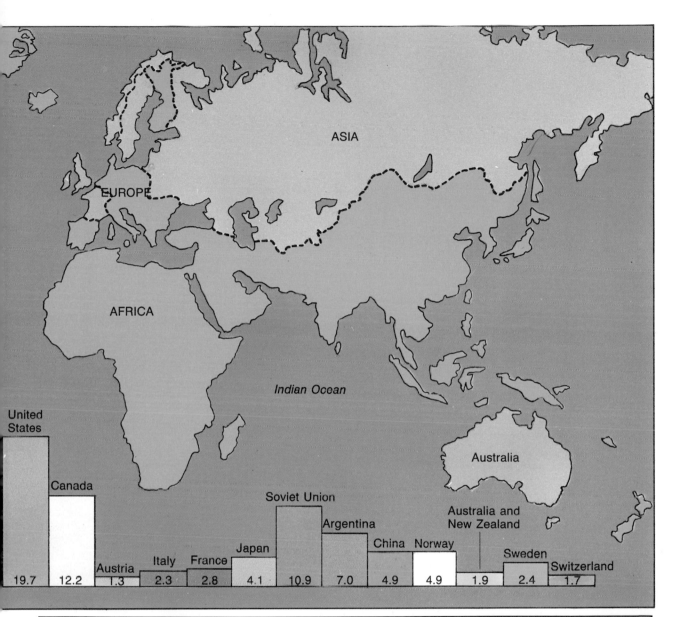

The bar graph shows values for:
- United States: 19.7
- Canada: 12.2
- Austria: 1.3
- Italy: 2.3
- France: 2.8
- Japan: 4.1
- Soviet Union: 10.9
- Argentina: 7.0
- China: 4.9
- Norway: 4.9
- Australia and New Zealand: 1.9
- Sweden: 2.4
- Switzerland: 1.7

The Highest, Biggest, Longest Dams in the World

	Name of dam	Country	Measurements	Type
Longest dam	Yacryeta-Apipe	Argentina and Paraguay	45 mi.	earth
Largest reservoirs	Bratsk	Soviet Union	44 million gals.	earth
	Aswan High Dam	Egypt	43.3 million gals.	earth
	Kariba	Zimbabwe	42 million gals.	concrete
	Akosombo	Ghana	39 million gals.	rock

25

Making Electricity

A hundred years ago people did not have electricity in their homes as we do today. People did not know what electricity could do.

The ancient Greeks were the first to find out about **static electricity.** When they rubbed a stone called amber on silk they found out that the stone could pick up pieces of dust.

In 1600 William Gilbert did experiments with iron filings and a **magnet.**

In 1881 Thomas Edison built the first power station that supplied power to homes in the United States.

In 1931 Michael Faraday showed that a magnet could produce electricity.

You can make electricity by rubbing a balloon against your sweater. When you let go of the balloon, static electricity will make it stick to the ceiling.

If you have a magnet, metal things will stick to one end, the **positive** end, but not to the other end, the **negative** end.

an ancient Greek experiments with static electricity

William Gilbert invented the word "electric" to describe how magnets attract things

Michael Faraday discovered how to produce electricity

Thomas Edison built an electricity generating station in New York

Power Stations

How a Hydroelectric Power Station Works

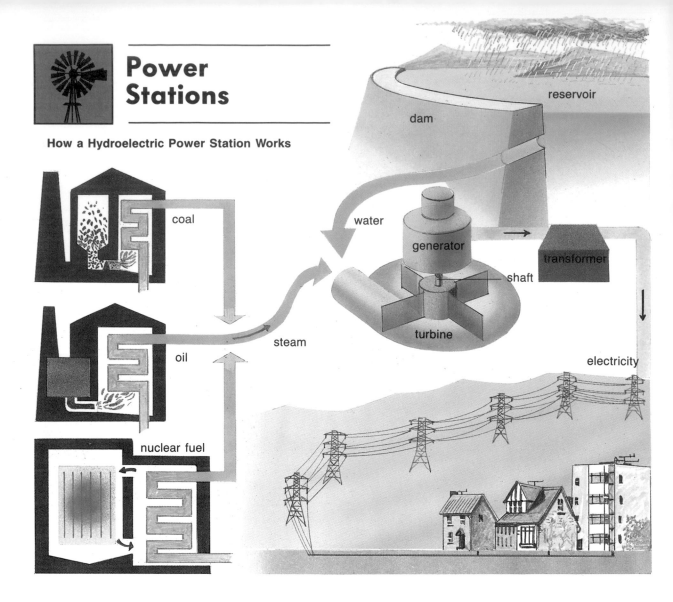

coal

water

generator

transformer

shaft

oil

steam

turbine

electricity

nuclear fuel

reservoir

dam

Besides water power, coal, oil, and nuclear fuel are all used in power stations to turn the turbines.

The spinning turbines turn a generator that makes the electric power.

A **transformer** changes the power so that it can be sent by cables to our houses.

28

the control
room in a
power
station

the Nurek
hydro-
electric
station in
the Soviet
Union.

Supply and Demand

Power stations generate electricity which travels along cables to where it will be used in our homes. The cables join together to make a **power grid.** At **peak** time such as the early evening, the power stations must generate more electricity to meet everyone's needs.

most homes have lots of electrical equipment

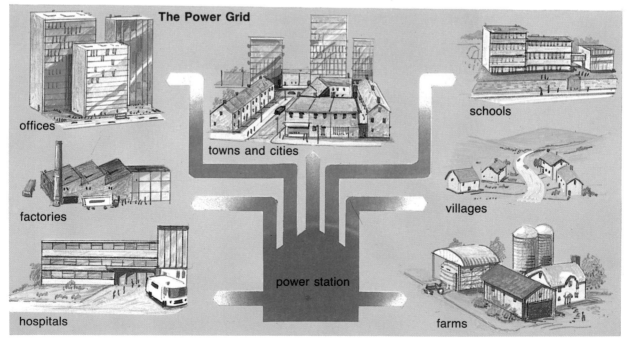

The Power Grid

offices

towns and cities

schools

factories

villages

hospitals

power station

farms

30

The cables are carried across the countryside on pylons. The flow of electricity along the cables is measured in **volts.** The turbines in most power stations generate electricity at a pressure of about 25,000 volts before the electricity is sent along the cables. The transformer lowers the pressure so that the electricity can be safely used in cities, towns, homes, and businesses. Electricity is used at higher pressures in factories than it is in **domestic** use.

Storing Energy

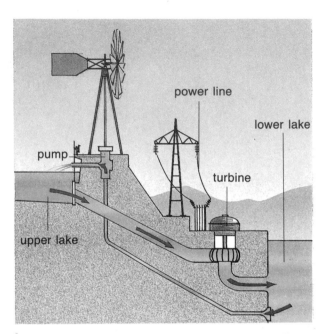

power line

lower lake

pump

turbine

upper lake

Oil can be stored in a tank until it is needed but we cannot store wind power or electricity that way.

Windmills make the most energy on windy days. Engineers use the extra electricity made on windy days to pump water from a lake up to a higher lake.

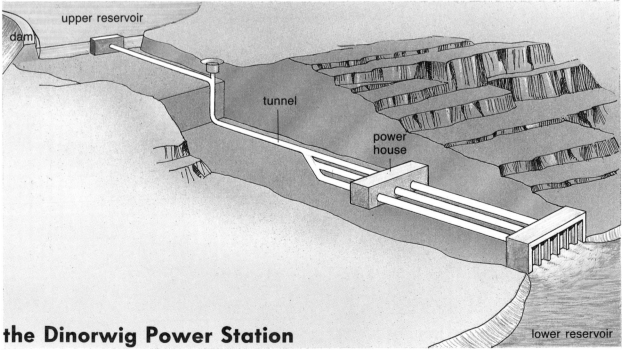

upper reservoir

dam

tunnel

power house

lower reservoir

the Dinorwig Power Station

The diagram and photo show the
Dinorwig Power Station in Wales.
Engineers use electricity to pump water
up to the upper reservoir late at night
when people need less electricity.
When more electricity is needed, water
rushes down the tunnel to turn the
turbines inside the power house.

Using River Power

**farmers planting rice in
flooded fields**

**water mills are turned
by the Danube River**

The world's rivers release a
huge amount of power in
the form of movement as
they flow down to the sea.
In China this water power is
used by 90,000 small
power stations built along
the riverbanks.

Farmers also use water
power to raise water from
the rivers for **irrigation.**

You can see how much energy and power
there is in a big river when it floods.
Floods often cause a lot of damage, but
they can be helpful as well.
When the Nile River flooded it left
rich mud which the Egyptian farmers
used to help them grow good crops.

Using the Tides

About 400 years ago there were many **tidal** mills along the coasts of Great Britain. They worked like water mills. At high tide the incoming seawater rushed through the sluice gates into a mill pond. At low tide the miller let the water from the pond flow back to the sea.

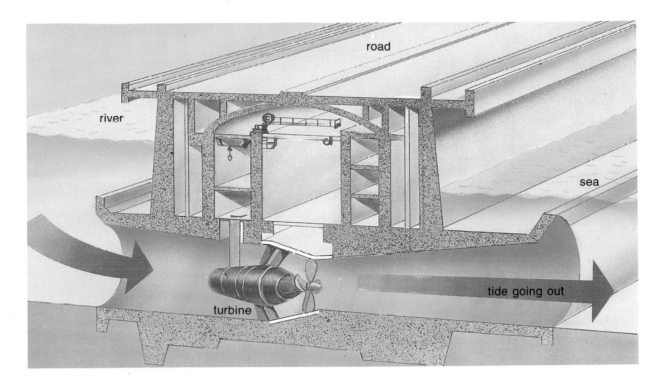

river

road

sea

tide going out

turbine

The diagram and picture show a tidal power station on the Rance River in France. It makes lots of electricity.

Engineers built a **barrage** at the place where the Rance River enters the sea. Its walls are very strong. At high tide the river level is 26 feet above the level at low tide. As the tide goes out the water turns the turbines in the Rance power station. When the tide comes in the water turns the turbines the other way.

Wave Power

The world's oceans are never still. **Currents** move huge quantities of water from one part of the ocean to another. Waves up to 80 feet high are formed. Scientists are working out how to use the power in these waves and currents.

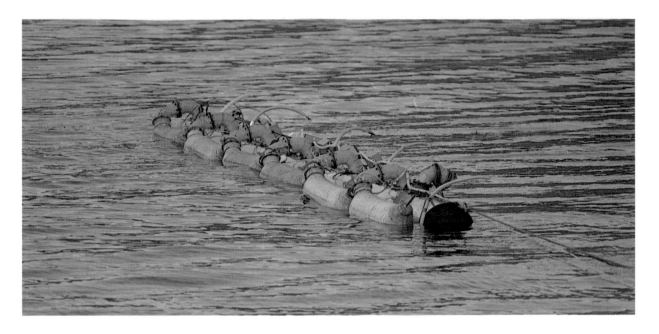

One experiment uses machines called
Salter Ducks that float on the sea.
A Salter Duck has flaps that move up
and down as the waves pass over them.
The flaps move a turbine to make
electricity.

Another experiment uses Cockerell
Rafts which are hinged in the middle.
These flap up and down with the waves
and force water through pumps.

Other scientists have built a tower
called an Oscillating Water Column.
The sea rushes in and out of it,
pushing the air inside up and down.
The moving air turns a special turbine.

Using the Wind

This wind generator at Howard's Knob, North Carolina, was once the largest in the world.

this was once the largest windmill in the world

The Howard's Knob wind generator had two huge blades like the propellers of an airplane. The windmill generated enough electricity to supply about 500 homes.

When groups of wind generators are built close to each other, they are called "wind farms." Wind farms are built in very windy places where few people live. Cables are then used to carry the electricity to towns and cities.

The wind farm in this picture is in California.

New Kinds of Energy

The horse in the picture uses the energy stored in the food he eats to help him pull the heavy cart.

Until about 50 years ago, farmers used horses to do the work that is now done by tractors. This is why energy in cars and trucks is sometimes measured in **horsepower.**

Today scientists are looking for ways to save energy. Ships with sails controlled by computers save fuel. These ships have special sails that are designed to turn to catch the winds.

Scientists also use Ocean Thermal Energy Convertors (OTECs) to make electricity. OTECs use energy on the warm surface of the ocean to boil liquid **ammonia.** The boiling ammonia gives off a gas that drives a turbine to make electricity.

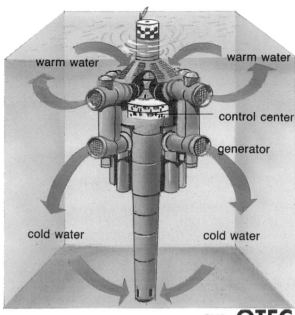

an OTEC

Cold water from the bottom of the ocean cools the gas so it turns back into liquid. Then the process can begin all over again.

a new kind of sailing ship

43

Looking Ahead

In some parts of the world, hot water bubbles up to the surface and can be used to generate electricity. Scientists are looking for other ways to use such geothermal power from hot rocks deep in the Earth.

Many people waste a lot of the energy we produce.

a wind generator in Spain

a geothermal power station in Australia

44

Scientists are afraid that we are using up all the **non-renewable** energy in fossil fuels. The picture shows the many kinds of renewable energy we could use instead.

Water and wind power cannot provide all the energy needed in the future, but if we did not waste so much energy, we would need less of it. Huge amounts of heat escape through walls, windows, and chimneys. We throw away more ''waste'' products like paper that can be used again. We can all help to save energy.

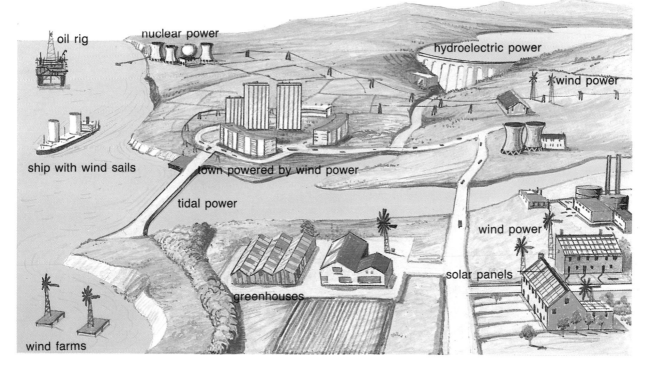

oil rig

nuclear power

hydroelectric power

wind power

ship with wind sails

town powered by wind power

tidal power

wind power

solar panels

greenhouses

wind farms

Glossary

ammonia   a colorless gas with a very strong smell which when cooled under pressure is easily changed into a liquid.

atmosphere   the layer of gases that surround the Earth.

barrage   a dam across a river.

currents   the movement of the water in the oceans, caused by winds.

domestic   used in houses and homes.

energy   the power that makes things move and work.

Equator   the imaginary circle around the middle of the Earth. The hottest parts of the world are at the Equator.

evaporate   to change from a liquid into a gas.

fossil fuels   materials like oil, coal, and gas that were made by the remains of tiny animals and plants millions of years ago.

foundations   the part of a building or structure that is buried in the ground.

generator   a machine for changing mechanical energy into electrical energy.

geothermal energy   a kind of energy that is produced using the heat from below the Earth's surface.

horizontal windmill   a windmill in which the sails go around level with, or parallel to the ground.

horsepower   a measurement of power. In the past people compared the power of a machine with the amount of work a single horse could do.

hurricane   a very violent tropical storm with high winds.

hydroelectric power   electricity that has been made by using fast-flowing water to drive a turbine.

irrigation   watering land that has too little rain by using a system of pipes and ditches.

magnet   a bar of iron that attracts other bits of metal.

millstone   a flat round stone used for crushing grain into flour.

negative   the end of a magnet that pushes away or repels iron filings.

non-renewable something that cannot be replaced.

nuclear power the power produced by heat when atoms are split.

peak the time when power stations have to produce the highest amount of electricity.

positive the end of a magnet that attracts or pulls iron filings toward it.

power grid the network of inter-connected cables across the country.

pylons tall steel frames or columns that support electricity cables above the ground.

renewable something that can be replaced or put back after being used.

reservoir a very large tank or lake where water is collected or stored.

shaft a long handle or pole in an engine that carries the power from the engine to the wheels.

sluice gates gates in a waterway that are used to control the flow of water going through.

solar power power from the Sun's rays that can be used to make electricity.

spillway a channel taking water away from a dam after it has been used.

static electricity an electric charge made by rubbing.

tidal depending on the tides rising and falling.

trade winds the winds that blow from the tropics toward the Equator.

transformer a machine that changes the force of an electric current.

transportation ways of getting from one place to another.

turbine a wheel that has many curved blades. It is spun around rapidly by the movement of gas or a liquid.

vapor tiny drops that form in the air when a liquid is heated.

vertical mills windmills where the sails turn around at right angles to the ground.

volt the measurement of the force of an electric current.

weir a low dam built across a river.

Index

Photographic credits
(t=top b=bottom l=left r=right)
cover: Science Photo Library. Tim Davis: **title page:** ZEFA
5 Alex Williams Seaphot; 9 Frank Lane Picture Library; 10, 11, 12. ZEFA; 14 Mansell Collection; 15t ZEFA; 15b The National Trust; 17 ZEFA; 18t South American Pictures; 18b, 21t ZEFA; 21b South American Pictures; 22 Peter Stevenson Seaphot; 23 British Columbian Embassy; 19t Fairclough Picture Library; 29b, 31 ZEFA; 33 Central Electricity Generating Board; 34t Chris Fairclough Picture Library; 34b South American Pictures; 35 David Refern/Seaphot; 36 South American Pictures; 37, 38 ZEFA; 39, 40 Science Photo Library; 41 Chris Fairclough Picture Library; 42 Frank Lane Picture Agency; 43 Japan Ship Company; 44t, 44b ZEFA